The Living Family

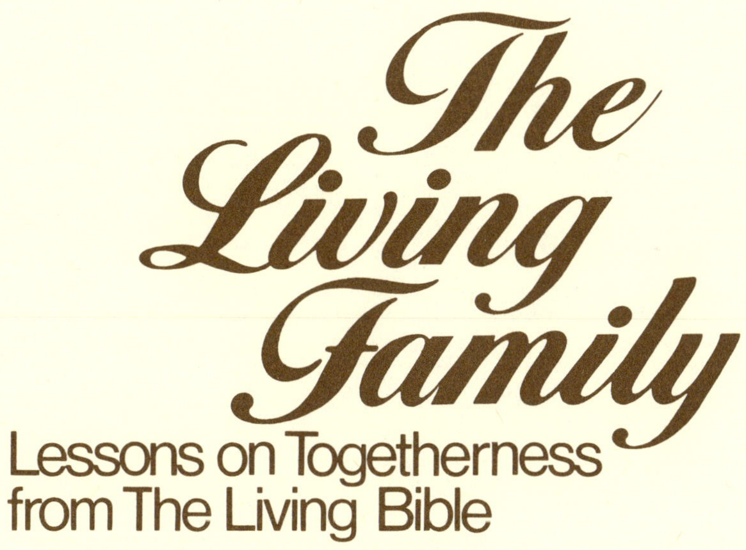

The Living Family

Lessons on Togetherness from The Living Bible

Ruth Rambo

FLEMING H. REVELL COMPANY

OLD TAPPAN, NEW JERSEY

Library of Congress Cataloging in Publication Data

Rambo, Ruth.
  The living family.

  Includes bibliographical references.
  1. Family—Religious life.   I. Title.
BV4526.2.R35   1984   249   83-8619
ISBN 0-8007-1378-8

CONTENTS

ACKNOWLEDGMENTS

Acknowledgment is made to the following for permission to reprint copyrighted material:

ABINGDON PRESS: Excerpts from *Mental Health Through Christian Community* by Howard Clinebell; excerpt by Theodore Roosevelt from *A Treasury of Sermon Illustrations*, edited by Charles Wallis; excerpt from IF I WERE STARTING MY FAMILY AGAIN by John Drescher. Copyright © 1979 by Abingdon. Used by permission. Reprinted by permission from the March 1979 issue of *Guideposts* magazine.

ALLYN AND BACON, INC.: Excerpt from CHILD DEVELOPMENT AND LEARNING by Harold W. Bernard Copyright © 1973 by Allyn and Bacon, Inc. Reprinted with permission.

BAKER BOOK HOUSE: Excerpts from *Christian Living in the Home* by Jay Adams. Copyright © 1972 by Jay Adams and used by permission of Baker Book House; excerpt from *Nurturing Children in the Lord* by Jack Fennema reprinted 1979 by Baker Book House and used by permission.

BETHANY HOUSE PUBLISHERS: Excerpt from THE CHRISTIAN FAMILY by Larry Christenson, published and copyright © 1978. Bethany House Publishers, Minneapolis, MN 55438.

BMH BOOKS: Excerpt from *The Family First* by Kenneth Gangel, BMH Books, Winona Lake, IN.

HENRY R. BRANDT AND HOMER E. DOWDY: Excerpts from *Building a Christian Home*.

GRACIE CHAPMAN: Excerpt from "His, Mine . . . Ours," as appeared in *Good Housekeeping* magazine, November 1982.

CHOSEN BOOKS: Excerpt from LET'S KEEP CHRISTMAS by Peter Marshall Copyright © 1953 by Catherine Marshall. Published by Chosen Books, Lincoln, VA 22078. Used by permission.

CHRISTIANITY TODAY MAGAZINE: Excerpt from "The Greatest Educational Force," by editorial staff, August 24, 1964, © 1964 by CHRISTIANITY TODAY and used by permission.

CROWN PUBLISHERS, INC.: Excerpts from LIMITS: A SEARCH FOR NEW VALUES by Maxine Schnall. Coyright © 1981 by Maxine Schnall. Used by permission of Clarkson N. Potter, Inc.

DIAL PRESS: Excerpt from *Bernard Meltzer's Guidance for Living* by Bernard Meltzer Copyright © 1982 by Mellan Associates, Inc. Permission Granted by The Dial Press.

DR. ALICE GINOTT: Excerpt from *Between Parent and Teenager* by Dr. Haim Ginott.

DR. FITZHUGH DODSON: Excerpt from *How to Father*, © by Dr. Fitzhugh Dodson.

INTRODUCTION

From beginning to end, *The Living Bible* contains references to the family. In the first chapter of Genesis, even before humankind's fall, the family as an institution was commanded by the Triune God. Further, God, the Originator of the nuclear family, also authored the written Revelation to instruct this earthbound family about life. All the necessary instructions for life within the family are included in *The Living Bible.* Families following His instructions are referred to as "living families" in this book.

The Living Family is meant to be both instruction and inspiration. The text speaks to questions concerning who and what makes a family. What is God's Word on nurture and discipline? What is the result of living in family as described by the Author of *The Living Bible?* Read the selected Scripture references for a reflection of God's view of the family.

You are invited to make this a standard for your home and family. Each idea or excerpt is a separate thought unit for you to ponder. None of the topics are considered comprehensive on the subject. There are some keys to successful family living; these keys may help you to lock out the pressures that would fragment and destroy the living family as described in God's Word.

And one might therefore
say of me that in this book I
have only made up a bunch of
other people's flowers, and that
of my own I have only provided the
string that ties them together.

MICHEL EYQUEM DE MONTAIGNE
Essays

FAMILY

Blessings on all who reverence and trust the Lord—on all who obey him! Their reward shall be prosperity and happiness. Your wife shall be contented in your home. And look at all those children! There they sit around the dinner table as vigorous and healthy as young olive trees. That is God's reward to those who reverence and trust him. May the Lord continually bless you with heaven's blessings as well as with human joys. May you live to enjoy your grandchildren! And may God bless Israel!

Psalms 128:1–6

THE FAMILY DEFINED AND DEFENDED

Families are combinations of marriage and new life. A sound decision as to whom to marry and when to plan for new life will assure a stronger family. These major decisions needing great wisdom are, ironically, made in the first third of a person's life. God's help, therefore, seems vital, and is available for both choosing a life partner and planning a family.

"The family is a cell of love, created by the lifelong friendship between a man and a woman, with complete sharing of body and mind, and with, normally, the procreation of children. The family is not sufficient unto itself; it is dependent upon and contributes to society, and while making possible the richest personality development of its individual members, it also prepares them to serve their fellow men and to live together with them in the wider family of humanity." [1]

"A family is a complex blending of relationships—an interaction of personalities, minds, and emotions. It is a living mobile . . . form and freedom. A family is an economic unit, a shelter, and a museum of memories." [2]

"So long as the human race continues, that is, so long as there are children, the family will be there as it has been." [3]

"Attempts to tamper with the family run into a specific problem. No one has the choice to be born or to be born into a specific family. People who wish to be independent and self-directed have to reckon with their own birth and childhood." [4]

"The healthy family is the womb of healthy personality, a haven of relatedness, the place above every other place where 'the heavenly bread of self being' is passed." [5]

"The family was ordained of God that children might be trained up for Himself; it was before the church, or rather the first form of the church on earth.

"Inasmuch as the domestic household is antecedent, as well in idea as in fact, to the fathering of men into community, the family must necessarily have rights and duties which are prior to those of the community and founded more immediately in nature." [6]

GOD'S ORIGINAL IDEA

Genesis 1:26–28

Then God said, "Let us make a man—someone like ourselves, to be the master of all life upon the earth and in the skies and in the seas."

 So God made man like his Maker.
 Like God did God make man;
 Man and maid did he make them.

And God blessed them and told them, "Multiply and fill the earth and subdue. . . ."

Genesis 2:18

And the Lord God said, "It isn't good for man to be alone; I will make a companion for him, a helper suited to his needs."

Genesis 4:1, 2

Then Adam had sexual intercourse with Eve his wife, and she conceived and gave birth to a son, Cain (meaning "I have created"). For, as she said, "With God's help, I have created a man!" Her next child was his brother, Abel.

Proverbs 8:27–31

"I was there when he established the heavens and formed the great springs in the depths of the oceans. I was there when he set the limits of the seas and gave them his instructions not to spread beyond their boundaries. I was there when he made the blueprint for the earth and oceans. I was always at his side like a little child. I was his constant delight, laughing and playing in his presence. And how happy I was with what he created—his wide world and all his family of mankind!"

Matthew 19:4–6

"Don't you read the Scriptures?" he replied. "In them it is written that at the beginning God created man and woman, and that a man should leave his father and mother, and be forever united to his wife. The two shall become one—no longer two, but one! And no man may divorce what God has joined together."

Ecclesiastes 4:9–11

Two can accomplish more than twice as much as one, for the results can be much better. If one falls, the other pulls him up; but if a man falls when he is alone, he's in trouble. Also, on a cold night, two under the same blanket gain warmth from each other, but how can one be warm alone?

The best friend of the family is God Himself. He was the Originator of this institution. There is universal patterning of the original plan. Every nation has the family.

"God makes the world all over again whenever a little child is born." [7]

The wonder of a new person coming from the total unity of two other persons seems enough to prove the existence of a Higher Being. One powerful argument for the existence of God is the birth of a new family. Human procreation is one of the greatest proofs of a great mind and heart behind the universe.

"The first contribution to the family heritage of the present day can be thought of as coming from the Hebrew patriarchal family. . . . For many centuries the Bible was a guide to living, and hence provided a model affecting family relationships. If a sacred book reflects a patriarchal age, a patriarchal pattern tends to permeate the family living of those guided by the sacred book. Our Puritan forefathers read their Bibles and acted accordingly. In log cabins on the frontier, biblical characters affected thinking about the family." [8]

Persons are born into their first family. Persons establish their second and future families. The more mature the decisions related to the second family, the greater the possibility for a significant family life—a living family.

GOD'S BLESSING AND REWARD

Psalms 112:1–3

Praise the Lord! For all who fear God and trust in him are blessed beyond expression. Yes, happy is the man who delights in doing his commands. His children shall be honored everywhere, for good men's sons have a special heritage. He himself shall be wealthy, and his good deeds will never be forgotten.

Psalms 128:1–6

Blessings on all who reverence and trust the Lord—on all who obey him! Their reward shall be prosperity and happiness. Your wife shall be contented in your home. And look at all those children! There they sit around the dinner table as vigorous and healthy as young olive trees. That is God's reward to those who reverence and trust him. May the Lord continually bless you with heaven's blessings as well as with human joys. May you live to enjoy your grandchildren! And may God bless Israel!

GOD'S LOVING-KINDNESS EXPRESSED

Oh, that these men would praise the Lord for his loving kindness and for all of his wonderful deeds! Let them praise him
publicly before the congregation, and before the leaders of
the nation. He dries up rivers, and turns the good land of the
wicked into deserts of salt. Again, he turns deserts into fertile,
watered valleys. He brings the hungry to settle there and
build their cities, to sow their fields and plant their vineyards,
and reap their bumper crops! How he blesses them! They
raise big families there, and many cattle. But others become
poor through oppression, trouble and sorrow. For God pours
contempt upon the haughty and causes princes to wander
among ruins; but he rescues the poor who are godly and gives
them many children and much prosperity. Good men everywhere will see it and be glad, while evil men are stricken si-
lent. Listen, if you are wise, to what I am saying. Think about
the lovingkindness of the Lord!

Psalms 107:31–43

Large families and many children are mentioned in this psalm as expres-
sive of God's loving-kindness. In the twentieth century, the Western world
has sought to balance perceived overpopulation with smaller families and
fewer children. This does not change the truth of this text, that God's loving-kindness is the root of both the family and children.

THE CHRISTIAN FAMILY IS A STRONG FORCE

The living family is often referred to as a "Christian family." The word *Christian* suggests that the family's belief system centers in Jesus Christ rather than in Buddha, Mohammed, or humanity alone. Further, some refer to a "strong Christian family" which implies a strong faith and a level of commitment to Christ that moderates individual and family activity.

"A Christian family is a regular family except that all the people in it are working together to help each other become everything God wants them to be." [9]

"A happy family is but an earlier heaven." [10]

"The Christian home is the Master's workshop where the processes of character molding are silently, lovingly, faithfully, and successfully carried on." [11]

"A truly Christian home is a place where sinners live, but with continual confession and rectifying of sin, there is growth by grace." [12]

"The secret of Christian family living is to cultivate the presence of Christ; it is living by a power beyond ourselves." [13]

"The Christian home is the womb of interpersonal relationships and reality." [14]

The family needs a nucleus (center, heart, a vibrant and dynamic organ around which the family moves and finds its identity). This definite "common other" to which all family members relate must be equal distance from each member. If it is first priority for one member and third for another, it affects the community or commonness of family life. Each family needs to specify or determine their common point, and fight elements that could splinter it.

"If your family is going to work, you have to *make* it work. . . . Identify your nucleus. If you don't have one, build one." [15]

"The secret to having a happy family—no matter how large or who belongs to whom—is in emphasizing the family and not the problems." [16]

BLESSING AND PUNISHMENT FROM GOD RELATE TO THE WHOLE FAMILY

"And when I punish people for their sins, the punishment continues upon the children, grandchildren, and great-grand-children of those who hate me; but I lavish my love upon thousands of those who love me and obey my commandments."

Exodus 20:5, 6

"May God prosper you and your family and multiply everything you own."

1 Samuel 25:6

When David saw the angel, he said to the Lord, "Look, I am the one who has sinned! What have these sheep done? Let your anger be only against me and my family."

2 Samuel 24:17

The Ark remained there with the family of Obededom for three months, and the Lord blessed him and his family.

1 Chronicles 13:14

But later on, the Lord will bring a terrible curse on you and on your nation and your family.

Isaiah 7:17

Jehovah is constantly thinking about us and he will surely bless us. He will bless the people of Israel and the priests of Aaron, and all, both great and small, who reverence him. May the Lord richly bless both you and your children. Yes, Jehovah who made heaven and earth will personally bless you!

Psalms 115:12–15

GOD'S PLAN TO CONTINUE THE UNIVERSAL FAMILY

Through Noah

Genesis 6:8	But Noah was a pleasure to the Lord.
Genesis 6:22	And Noah did everything as God commanded him.
Genesis 7:7	He boarded the boat with his wife and sons and their wives, to escape the flood.

Through Abram

Genesis 17:1–4

"I am the Almighty; obey me and live as you should. I will prepare a contract between us, guaranteeing to make you into a mighty nation. In fact you shall be the father of not only one nation, but a multitude of nations!" Abram fell face downward in the dust as God talked with him.

Genesis 17:6

"I will give you millions of descendants who will form many nations! . . ."

Genesis 17:7, 8

"And I will continue this agreement between us generation after generation, forever, for it shall be between me and your children as well. It is a contract that I shall be your God and the God of your posterity. . . ."

Through Joshua

Joshua 4:21, 22

Then Joshua explained again the purpose of the stones: "In the future," he said, "when your children ask you why these stones are here and what they mean, you are to tell them that these stones are a reminder of this amazing miracle. . . ."

Joshua 4:24

"He did this so that all the nations of the earth will realize that Jehovah is the mighty God, and so that all of you will worship him forever."

Joshua 24:14, 15

"So revere Jehovah and serve him in sincerity and truth. . . . But as for me and my family, we will serve the Lord."

"We are witnesses. May the Lord make this woman, who has
now come into your home, as fertile as Rachel and Leah, from
whom all the nation of Israel descended!"

Ruth 4:11

He was the father of Jesse and grandfather of King David.

Ruth 4:17

". . . And the Lord God shall give him the throne of his ances-
tor David. And he shall reign over Israel forever; his Kingdom
shall never end!"

Luke 1:32, 33

PARENTS

"... Are they *my* children? Am I their father? Is that why you have given me the job of nursing them along like babies until we get to the land you promised their ancestors?"

Numbers 11:12

I will comfort you there as a little one is comforted by its mother.

Isaiah 66:13

"The first ingredient for a happy family is a well put-together mother and father."[1]

> The most important thing
> that a father can do for his children
> is to love their mother.
>
> And conversely,
> the most important thing
> that a mother can do for her children
> is to love their father.[2]

Divorce is no threat to two persons who work at a growing relationship—who live as if they love each other, whether or not they happen to be feeling romantic at the moment. Love is something you are to another. Divorce or separation, therefore, shakes your personhood.

"There is no question that the family is the primary shaper of values. . . ."[3]

"The less care a child has in the early years, the more society will pay for it later on."[4]

"The chief job of the home is to train family members to live fruitfully in home, church, and society."[5]

"Beyond everything else my parents did right, they did this: they trusted God.

"Their God was big enough to keep their children, so they need not run their lives."[6]

GOD'S SOVEREIGNTY COMFORTS PARENTS

Romans 11:33–36

Oh, what a wonderful God we have! How great are his wisdom and knowledge and riches! How impossible it is for us to understand his decisions and his methods! For who among us can know the mind of the Lord? Who knows enough to be his counselor and guide? And who could ever offer to the Lord enough to induce him to act? For everything comes from God alone. Everything lives by his power, and everything is for his glory. To him be glory evermore.

"All the works and doings of God are wonderful, but none more awful than His great work of election and reprobation; when we consider how many good parents have had bad children, and again how many bad parents have had pious children, it should make us adore the sovereignty of God, who will not be tied to time nor place, nor yet to persons, but takes and chooses, when and where and whom He pleases; it should also teach the children of godly parents to walk with fear and trembling, lest they through unbelief fall short of a promise; it may also be a support to such as have or had wished parents that if they abide not in unbelief, God is able to gaff them in." [7]

GOD, THE FATHER, ALSO IDENTIFIES WITH PARENTS

"... Are they *my* children? Am I their father? Is that why you have given me the job of nursing them along like babies until we get to the land you promised their ancestors?"   Numbers 11:12

And the Lord replies: Ephraim is still my son, my darling child. I had to punish him, but I still love him. I long for him and surely will have mercy on him.   Jeremiah 31:20

"Listen to me, all Israel who are left; I have created you and cared for you since you were born. I will be your God through all your lifetime, yes, even when your hair is white with age. I made you and I will care for you. . . ."   Isaiah 46:3, 4

I will comfort you there as a little one is comforted by its mother.   Isaiah 66:13

THE ROLE OF PARENTS INCLUDES DISCIPLINE

Proverbs 13:24

If you refuse to discipline your son, it proves you don't love him; for if you love him you will be prompt to punish him.

Proverbs 19:18

Discipline your son in his early years while there is hope. If you don't you will ruin his life.

Proverbs 20:30

Punishment that hurts chases evil from the heart.

Proverbs 22:15

A youngster's heart is filled with rebellion, but punishment will drive it out of him.

Proverbs 23:13, 14

Don't fail to correct your children; discipline won't hurt them! They won't die if you use a stick on them! Punishment will keep them out of hell.

Proverbs 29:15, 17

Scolding and spanking a child helps him to learn. Left to himself, he brings shame to his mother.... Discipline your son and he will give you happiness and peace of mind.

Proverbs 29:19

Sometimes mere words are not enough—discipline is needed. For the words may not be heeded.

Hebrews 12:7–11

Let God train you, for he is doing what any loving father does for his children. Whoever heard of a son who was never corrected? If God doesn't punish you when you need it, as other fathers punish their sons, then it means that you aren't really God's son at all—that you don't really belong in his family. Since we respect our fathers here on earth, though they punish us, should we not all the more cheerfully submit to God's training so that we can begin really to live? Our earthly fathers trained us for a few brief years, doing the best for us that they knew how, but God's correction is always right and for our best good, that we may share his holiness. Being punished isn't enjoyable while it is happening—it hurts! But afterwards we can see the result, a quiet growth in grace and character.

"Discipline with dignity requires work. It includes a few enforced rules and the united authority of both parents." [8]

"The scriptural method of discipline is by the rod. The rod is the way of love. It is the first response, not the last resort. It works. God appointed it." [9]

"Respectful and responsible children result from families where a proper combination of love and discipline is present.

"Developing respect for the parent is the critical factor in child management.

"Punishment is not something one does to the child but for the child." [10]

"Discipline moves from enforced discipline to self-discipline to Christ discipline." [11]

> Let love be supreme.
> Explain your convictions.
> Live your convictions consistently.
> Feed your children responsibility.
> Houseclean your attitudes.
> Seek God's will, not your own. [12]

"You can punish any child you have the right and strength to punish. You can only discipline those children who choose to be your disciples; that is who follow you, pattern after you, love and respect you.

"Only the parents who give real listening presence—who give time and attention to their children—can qualify to give discipline.

"The Bible puts it this way: 'As children copy their fathers so you should copy the Lord Christ and both of you will grow toward true maturity.' " [13]

"Seeing children as they are seen in the Word of God helps us to perceive their worth, their potential, their individuality, and *their need of parental authority*—all from a higher-than-human point of view." [14]

"Parental authority is to teach a child respect for other authority. In God's dealings with man, there is a clear distinction between punishment as a means of administering just retribution for misdeeds, and discipline which is designed to promote the growth of the disciplined one." [15]

EFFECTIVE PARENTING DEMANDS THE BEST FROM A MAN OR WOMAN

"Nature teaches us to love our children as ourselves." [16]

"The best prepared, the most hyper-planned of us, still find that parenting is twenty years of on-the-job training." [17]

"The hardest job of parenting has been the letting go of our children.
"The last function of good parenting is that of becoming a base for your child's returning." [18]

"Parents, oh! How much ought you to be continually devising and even travailing, for the good of your children. Often devise, how to make them wise children; how to carry on a desirable education that shall render them desirable; how to render them lovely, and polite creatures, and serviceable in this generation. Often devise, how to enrich their minds with valuable knowledge; how to instill generous and gracious, and heavenly principles into their minds; how to restrain and rescue them from the paths of the Destroyer." [19]

"Let parents bequeath to their children not riches, but the spirit of reverence." [20]

"If I were asked what single qualification were necessary for one who has the care of children, I should say patience—patience with their tempers, with their misunderstandings, with their progress." [21]

PARENTS ARE THE PRIMARY INFLUENCE IN A CHILD'S LIFE

"Parents perpetuate their lives in their posterity and their manners; in their imitation children do naturally follow the failings [rather] than the virtues of their predecessors. . . ." [22]

"Parents do not usually set out deliberately to indoctrinate their children with the sorts of attitudes toward the world that the parents would like the children to have; yet, for all practical purposes indoctrination is precisely what does take place in most families.
"A child tends to emulate or imitate those adults who occupy large chunks of his life span." [23]

"In maintaining the organic unity of the family, I mean to assert that a power [is] exerted by parents over children, not only when they teach, encourage, persuade, and govern, but without any purposed control whatever. The bond is so intimate that they do it unconsciously and undesignedly— they must do it. Their character, feelings, spirit, and principles must propagate themselves, whether they will or not." [24]

> In part, we are born;
> In part, we are made;
> In part, we make ourselves. [25]

In times of stress, particularly during the teenage years, a parent wishes that the above were not true. It would be so much easier on one's ego and reputation to be able to make the decisions that determine the destiny of the young person. The parent comes closest perhaps to identifying with the heavenly Father at this point. He can see just what is best for us—the path we should take and why. We, too, can see just what is best for our children—the path they should choose and why. Here the similarity ends, however, because God knows the whole future and parents do not. Here we face the limits of parenting. Here we need the caution to avoid interference. Yet, how good it feels to be consulted!

> You may give them your love but not your thoughts,
> For they have their own thoughts.
> You may house their bodies but not their souls,
> For their souls dwell in the house of tomorrow, which you
>   cannot visit, not even in your dreams.
> You may strive to be like them, but seek not to make them like you.
> For life goes not backward nor tarries with yesterday.
> You are the bows from which your children as living arrows
>   are sent forth. [26]

PARENTS: BUILDERS THROUGH MODELING AND TEACHING

"... of all the teachers, the teaching function of the parent is most important and most influential. The most influential teachers, whether they realize it or not, are our parents." [27]

"The mother's heart is the child's schoolroom." [28]

"If a child has unforgiving parents he is likely to see God as unforgiving. If he has perfectionistic parents he will probably have difficulty believing God is ever pleased with his performance. And if he has a nagging parent he will tend to view God as being constantly 'on his back.' I believe confusion of God and parent is one of the major causes of spiritual rebellion among adolescents." [29]

"Children have a strange way of living up to your high opinion of them. And the reverse is true. If you keep telling a child he's no good—he'll prove you are right." [30]

"The humanness and identity of a child are developed within the family matrix. Each family has a unique emotional climate which, though constantly in flux, provides the psychological environment within which personality develops. . . . In the give-and-take of day-to-day family interaction the personhood of the child emerges and is molded by the family organism." [31]

"I believe *the* most valuable contribution a parent can make to his child is to instill in him a genuine faith in God.
"What a beautiful philosophy with which to 'clothe' your tender child.
"This is self-esteem at its richest, not dependent on the whims of birth or social judgment, or the cult of the superchild, but on divine decree." [32]

"Some parents are too busy in their own world to really get close to their children, but then there are also others who keep themselves busy in order to avoid getting close enough to have to share their real values." [33]

Messages that they do not have time for us are sent by teenagers in response to the messages which we sent to them when they were children.

> And my greatest joy is knowing that my children walk in truth,
> And that they are giving You, Lord, of their fire and strength of
> youth.
> Yes, I found that the joy of my salvation,
> Is knowing that my children walk in truth. [34]

FATHERS

Where is the man who fears the Lord? God will teach him how to choose the best. He shall live within God's circle of blessing, and his children shall inherit the earth. Friendship with God is reserved for those who reverence him. With them alone he shares the secrets of his promises.

Psalms 25:12–14

FATHERS WHO PLEASE GOD GIVE PRIORITY TO THEIR FAMILIES

Provider

And to Adam, God said, "Because you listened to your wife and ate the fruit when I told you not to, I have placed a curse upon the soil. All your life you will struggle to extract a living from it. It will grow thorns and thistles for you, and you shall eat its grasses. All your life you will sweat to master it, until your dying day. Then you will return to the ground from which you came. For you were made from the ground, and to the ground you will return."

Genesis 3:17–19

But anyone who won't care for his own relatives when they need help, especially those living in his own family, has no right to say he is a Christian. Such a person is worse than the heathen.

1 Timothy 5:8

Encourager

Fathers, don't scold your children so much that they become discouraged and quit trying.

Colossians 3:21

The fool who provokes his family to anger and resentment will finally have nothing worthwhile left. He shall be the servant of a wiser man.

Proverbs 11:29

Authority

Where is the man who fears the Lord? God will teach him how to choose the best. He shall live within God's circle of blessing, and his children shall inherit the earth. Friendship with God is reserved for those who reverence him. With them alone he shares the secrets of his promises.

Psalms 25:12–14

Reverence for God gives a man deep strength; his children have a place of refuge and security. Reverence for the Lord is a fountain of life. . . .

Proverbs 14:26, 27

And when we obey him, every path he guides us on is fragrant with his lovingkindness and his truth.

Psalms 25:10

Ephesians 5:1   Follow God's example in everything you do just as a much
                         loved child imitates his father.

1 Timothy 3:4, 5   He must have a well-behaved family, with children who obey
                         quickly and quietly. For if a man can't make his own little
                         family behave, how can he help the whole church?

1 Timothy 3:12   Deacons should have only one wife and they should have
                         happy, obedient families.

THE FATHER'S ROLE IS A DEMANDING YET PRIVILEGED ONE

If I Were Starting My Family Again:

I would love my wife more.
(I now know that there is a close relationship between
parents' love for each other and the child's obedi-
ence, love, and caring.)
I would laugh more with my children.
(As Oscar Wilde wrote, "The best way to make children
good is to make them happy.")
I would be a better listener.
I would seek to be more honest.
I would stop praying for my family.
(Something happened when I wanted God to change me
more than I wanted Him to change others.)
I would try for more togetherness.
I would do more encouraging.
(If I were starting my family again I would seek to be
more free to express words of appreciation and
praise.)
I would pay more attention to little things.
I would seek to develop feelings of belonging.
I would seek to share God more intimately.

If I Were Starting My Family Again.[1]

The father says, "I'm home a lot—more than most men." Sometimes a man prides himself on being home often. He sees that as taking
care of his fatherly obligations.

There is so much more to being a father and to giving to the family.
Just being in one's lounge chair or sitting at the head of the dinner
table is not ultimately satisfying for the wife and children. Then what
is satisfying and productive?

First, the wife and children need to know they are being planned
for. Second, being told of the plans or discussing the plans is important. Hustling the family about at the last frantic moment with instructions isn't good. Third, the father needs to find the signals and
small things that speak *caring* to each family member. Unfortunately,
many men are never aware of the language of caring. One who is
aware has the joy of touching the strings of a lovely instrument and
seeing response in the beauty and harmony produced.

Actually, these principles hold true for any quality human relationship.

"Any man can be a father, but it takes someone special to be a
dad."[2]

FATHERING IS A LEARNED PRIVILEGE

"No one is born a good father. To be a good father is a matter of patience, study, and love. But is is also a matter of information! It's important to learn everything you can about two basic subjects: child psychology and teaching methods." [3]

"By profession I am a soldier and take pride in that fact. But I am prouder, infinitely prouder to be a father. A soldier destroys in order to build. The father only builds, never destroys. The one has the potentialities of death; the other embodies creation and life. And while the hordes of death are mighty, the battles of life are mightier still. My hope is that my son, when I am gone, will remember me not from the battle, but in the home, repeating with him one simple daily prayer, "Our Father which art in heaven." [4]

> He teaches patience—by being gentle and understanding
>   over and over.
> He teaches honesty—by keeping his promises to his family
>   even when it costs.
> He teaches courage—by living unafraid, with faith,
>   in all circumstances.
> He teaches justice—by being fair and dealing equally
>   with everyone.
> Every father can teach Christian principles.
> He teaches kindness—by being thoughtful and gracious
>   even at home. [5]

"God set us a perfect example of fatherhood to follow. . . . A father's role is not an easy one. . . . We must understand the many hats dad wears. . . . He is to be the leader. . . . God's authority in the home centers in dad. He is to be a lover. . . . He must love his wife with an unselfish, forgiving love, a love that transcends all loves but that for Christ himself. . . . The third major role a father must play is that of disciplinarian. . . . The fourth role God would have every father fill is that of companion . . . by companion I mean comrade, confidant, and friend.

"Isn't this too much for one mere mortal to be and do? Yes, it is. The demands on his time will be relentless. The drain on his emotional resources will be unending. But the last role God requires of a Christian father will provide him with the strength to become everything else God wants him to be. He must be a man of God." [6]

"Blessed is he whose home is built upon the Word of God, for his roof will be shingled with happiness and all who pass by will see the goodness of the Lord." [7]

MOTHERS

Can a mother forget her little child and not have love
for her own son?

Isaiah 49:15

" 'Like mother, like daughter'—that is what everyone
will say of you."

Ezekiel 16:44

A MOTHER'S RESPONSES AND ROLE

Lord, how you have helped me before! You took me safely from my mother's womb and brought me through the years of infancy. I have depended upon you since birth. . . .

Psalms 22:9, 10, 11

I am quiet now before the Lord, just as a child who is weaned from the breast. . . .

Psalms 131:2

A worthy wife is her husband's joy and crown; the other kind corrodes his strength and tears down everything he does.

Proverbs 12:4

A wise woman builds her house, while a foolish woman tears hers down by her own efforts.

Proverbs 14:1

A sensible son gladdens his father. A rebellious son saddens his mother.

Proverbs 15:20

Can a mother forget her little child and not have love for her own son? . . .

Isaiah 49:15

" 'Like mother, like daughter'—that is what everyone will say of you."

Ezekiel 16:44

. . . She had heard about Jesus and now she came and fell at his feet, and pled with him to release her child from the demon's control. . . . And when she arrived home, her little girl was lying quietly in bed, and the demon was gone.

Mark 7:25, 26, 30

MOTHERHOOD, AN HONOR WITH RESPONSIBILITY ATTACHED

"Motherhood is undoubtedly one of the most complex and exacting callings in life. A poll among women revealed overwhelming agreement that raising children properly requires as much intelligence and drive as holding a top position in business and government. And that task falls mainly on the mother's shoulders for the first six years of the child's life." [1]

"When Eve was brought unto Adam, he became filled with the Holy Spirit, and gave her the most sanctified, the most glorious appellations. He called her Eve, that is to say, the Mother of All. He did not style her wife, but simply mother—mother of all living creatures. In this consists the glory and the most precious ornament of woman." [2]

"Observe how soon, and to what a degree, a mother's influence begins to operate! Her first ministration for her infant is to enter, as it were, the valley of the shadow of death, and win its life at the peril of her own! How different must an affection thus founded be from all others!" [3]

"Youth fades; love droops, the leaves of friendship fall;
A mother's secret hope outlives them all." [4]

Blessing she is,
God made her so,
And deeds of weekday holiness
Fall from her
Noiseless as the snow.[5]

"If I am Thy child, O God, it is because Thou didst give me such a mother." [6]

" 'What is wanting,' said Napoleon one day to Madame Campan, 'in order that the youth of France be well educated?'
" 'Good mothers,' was the reply. The emperor was most forcibly struck with this answer. 'Here,' said he, 'is a system in one word.' " [7]

"All that I am or hope to be, I owe to my angel mother." [8]

"She broke the bread into two fragments, and gave them to the children, who ate with avidity. 'She hath kept none for herself,' grumbled the sergeant. 'Because she is not hungry,' said a soldier. 'Because she is a mother,' said the sergeant." [9]

MOTHERING: A UNIQUE ATTACHMENT

To Daughters

I watch you come and go, my daughter. Now it's spring and you're restless. A knock at our door, a young voice, and you're like one transported into another world—away from me. A world of friends and fantasy whisked you away.

But you'll be back. I have my moments with you, too, to listen and to care. Never scheduled and rarely convenient are these moments. I don't call you as your friends do. If I wait, and go about my tasks, in your time, you'll come back to talk. Often more talk of hurt than joy, but that's all right for mothers. As long as you come back.

To Sons

"There is an enduring tenderness in the love of a mother to a son that transcends all other affections of the heart. It is neither to be chilled by selfishness, nor daunted by danger, nor weakened by worthlessness, nor stifled by ingratitude. She will sacrifice every comfort to his convenience; she will surrender every pleasure to his enjoyment; she will glory in his fame and exult in his prosperity; and if adversity overtake him, he will be dearer to her by misfortune; and if disgrace settle upon his name, she will still love and cherish him; and if all the world beside cast him off, she will be all the world to him." [10]

CHILDREN

Children are a gift from God; they are his reward. Children born to a young man are like sharp arrows to defend him. Happy is the man who has his quiver full of them. That man shall have the help he needs when arguing with his enemies.

Psalms 127:3–5

CHILDREN

Children are a gift from God; they are his reward. Children born to a young man are like sharp arrows to defend him. Happy is the man who has his quiver full of them. That man shall have the help he needs when arguing with his enemies.

Psalms 127:3–5

Your wife shall be contented in your home. And look at all those children! There they sit around the dinner table as vigorous and healthy as young olive trees. That is God's reward to those who reverence and trust him.

Psalms 128:3, 4

May the Lord continually bless you with heaven's blessings as well as with human joys. May you live to enjoy your grandchildren! . . .

Psalms 128:5, 6

The character of even a child can be known by the way he acts—whether what he does is pure and right.

Proverbs 20:11

Teach a child to choose the right path, and when he is older he will remain upon it.

Proverbs 22:6

About that time the disciples came to Jesus to ask which of them would be greatest in the Kingdom of Heaven! Jesus called a small child over to him and set the little fellow down among them, and said, "Unless you turn to God from your sins and become as little children, you will never get into the Kingdom of Heaven. Therefore anyone who humbles himself as this little child, is the greatest in the Kingdom of Heaven. And any of you who welcomes a little child like this because you are mine, is welcoming me and caring for me. But if any of you causes one of these little ones who trusts in me to lose his faith, it would be better for you to have a rock tied to your neck and be thrown into the sea."

Matthew 18:1–6

THE RIGHTS OF CHILDREN

"We affirm that children, natural and adopted, are a heritage from God, given in sacred trust. They are not to be abused or neglected. Children are not pawns of the Church, state, or parents. Every child deserves to have a warm, caring relationship with a mother and father, the opportunity to develop a healthy self-esteem through loving parents, and the opportunity to be nurtured in an environment which models Christian behavior and values.

"We believe that the roles of parents include providing for their children's growth (mentally, physically, spiritually, and socially), and teaching them from the Word of God in a spirit of Christian love and nurture. Parents, together, are responsible to teach spiritual truth and other information by word of mouth and by example. They are to discipline in a firm, consistent, loving manner in the home." [1]

"Children benefit from realizing that they provide parents with a specially vigorous viewpoint on life, a particularly spontaneous joy in living, and a delightfully reasonable excuse for such adults to react to life as children themselves once again." [2]

"Children have more need of models than of critics." [3]

"With children we must mix gentleness with firmness.

"They must not always have their own way, but they must not always be thwarted.

"If we never have headaches through rebuking them, we shall have plenty of heartaches when they grow up.

"Be obeyed at all costs; for if you yield up your authority once, you will hardly get it again." [4]

"The first duty to children is to make them happy. If you have not made them so, you have wronged them. No other good they may get can make up for that." [5]

"In the man whose childhood has known caresses and kindness, there is always a fibre of memory that can be touched to gentle issues." [6]

"What the best and wisest parent wants for his own child, that must the community want for all its children." [7]

"Lord, give to men who are old and rougher the things that little children suffer, and let's keep bright and undefiled the young years of the little child." [8]

Many psychologists believe that the same individual and social mechanisms operate in all children in all cultures. These mechanisms are the impetus for growth. The four basic mechanisms are: "(1) the desire to obtain affection, regard, acceptance, and recognition from others, and its corollary: (2) the wish to avoid the unpleasant feelings that occur when one is rejected or punished by others; (3) the desire to be like specific people whom the child has grown to respect, admire, or love (called identification); and (4) a tendency to imitate the actions of others." [9]

"As the world of work has changed drastically in recent decades, significant changes have also taken place in family life. . . . The modern family differs greatly from the family of a century ago. At one time the family had functions of protection, education, training for work, and religious formation. Other institutions of society have developed which now provide these services for children. One of the only remaining functions of the family with regard to children is socialization into the values of the society. Yet even in this function the family may be losing ground to media and peer groups." [10]

THE INFLUENCE OF CHILDREN

"What is the effect of being with children? By the pity, by the tenderness, by the peculiar modes of admiration which connect themselves with the helplessness, the innocence, the simplicity of children, not only are the primal affections strengthened and continually renewed, but the qualities which are dearest in the sight of heaven—the frailty, for instance, which appeals to forbearance, the innocence which symbolizes the heavenly, and the simplicity which is so alien from the worldly—are kept in perpetual remembrance, and their ideals are continually refreshed." [11]

"Children, who play life, discern its true law and revelations more clearly than men, who fail to live it worthily, but who think that they are wiser by experience, that is, by failure." [12]

> A child more than all other gifts
> That earth can offer to declining man,
> Brings hope with it, and forward looking thoughts. [13]

"Children are the anchors that hold a mother to life." [14]

"What gift has Providence bestowed on man that is so dear to him as his children?" [15]

"Children sweeten labors, but they make misfortunes more bitter. They increase the cares of life, but they mitigate the remembrance of death." [16]

"A harmonious intimacy between grandparents and grandchildren can very often be an incomparably precious blessing for both. . . . The development of grown-up children is a great experience, and grandchildren are a very special gift and a task. . . . The old need the young as much as the children need the old. . . . There are times when a child 'may need to have "only child" treatment and this can be given if there are grandparents available.' " [17]

"The value of real estate, gold, silver, and precious jewels can be computed in monetary terms. But who would place a price tag on a child? Yet it is tragically true that this most priceless member of the home is frequently the most neglected. This may be true even when much attention is given to better food and clothes, ventilation, and physical care. All these are necessary, but there is one need that goes deeper than any of these, and in this field is found striking criminal negligence; that is, the spiritual development of the child." [18]

NURTURING CHILDREN IN THE HOME

"But children, too, are created by God. Their origin is the same as that of the created reality in which they are instructed. Truth, reality, and children all originate from the same Source. This fact has great significance for Christian teachers and parents. Not only should they be looking to God and his Word for guidance on the instruction which is to be provided, but they must also look to God's Word to understand the children for whom the instruction and correction is intended. Since reality and children were created by God, they are meant to interact and interrelate in a harmonious manner." [19]

"The age of understanding and accountability is reached when the pieces of the pattern or big picture fit together or seem to make sense. At that point he becomes fully accountable before God for the response he makes to the claims of Christ on his life." [20]

Most adults spend a great deal of their adult lives trying to change their misconceptions of God. Concepts built about God in the early years of instruction are so fixed that they are difficult to change. The wise parent will continually attempt to see God through the eyes of the child and add "precept upon precept" so that only true concepts are built. This requires a great deal of listening to the child to understand what the child is seeing.

Since each child is unique, each has his or her own view of reality. Parenting is the ominous task that it is because of the need to construct along with the child a view of reality that is God-centered. However, the parent need not feel discouraged or inadequate. Children also bear the image of God and have an inner drive to know the truth.

"The Bible makes it clear that we should set limits on our children's actions.

"As parents we should sit down and logically establish necessary rules for our children's protection. Since having too many rules is frustrating, we should also see what rules can be eliminated. It is more important for a child to develop wholesome attitudes than ideal behavior.

"By treating our children as valuable people, we do much to lay the foundation for a healthy self-image." [21]

"There are many ways to discipline a child, but none of them can be completely effective until you have resolved your own frustrations." [22]

HOME

"Whenever you enter a city or village, search for a godly man and stay in his home until you leave for the next town. When you ask permission to stay, be friendly, and if it turns out to be a godly home, give it your blessing. . . ."

Matthew 10:11–13

U. S.
MAIL
APPROVED BY THE
POSTMASTER GENERAL

MORE THAN A PLACE TO LIVE

"Whenever you enter a city or village, search for a godly man and stay in his home until you leave for the next town. When you ask permission to stay, be friendly, and if it turns out to be a godly home, give it your blessing. . . ."

Matthew 10:11–13

If anyone comes to teach you, and he doesn't believe what Christ taught, don't even invite him into your home. . . .

2 John 1:10

You must teach [these commandments] to your children and talk about them when you are at home or out for a walk; at bedtime and the first thing in the morning. Tie them on your finger, wear them on your forehead, and write them on the doorposts of your house!

Deuteronomy 6:7, 8

THE LIVING FAMILY NEEDS A NEST

"The environment for a family is the home, not only the physical surroundings that in themselves call for tremendous effort to develop, but in the culture that enlivens it." [1]

"Hard indeed, is a world which has come to feel that it is more important to have an automobile to get away from home with than to have a home which you might like to stay in." [2]

"The Christian home is the Master's workshop where the processes of character molding are silently, lovingly, faithfully, and successfully carried on." [3]

Home was almost sacrosanct for leaders in the seventeenth and eighteenth centuries. Pestalozzi wrote that "our home joys are the most delightful earth affords." Washington Irving said that he valued "this delicious home-feeling as one of the choicest gifts a parent can bestow."

" 'Home' is the only place in society where we can now connect along the ages, like discs along the spine of society! The only place where we remember that we're related, and that's not a bad idea to go home to." [4]

Judaism has always put the major responsibility for the child's moral and spiritual development in the home. The home is "the nursery of religion and of morality as well as of culture. No other influence may compare with the home for the lasting and far-reaching effects upon the child's development." [5]

"The first essential for a man's being a good citizen is his possession of the home virtues, based on recognition of the great underlying laws of religion and morality. No piled up wealth, no splendor of material growth, no brilliance of artistic development, will permanently avail any people unless its home life is healthy." [6]

"To be happy at home is the ultimate result of all ambition." [7] Persons not happy at home seem to express a fragmentation in their being.

THE CHRISTIAN HOME IS MANY THINGS

When newlyweds begin to construct the image of home into which they will bring infants, a proper idea is important. It is not merely a boarding-house or architect's creation. It can be a private chapel. It must be a refuge from the stress of life. Daily classes in Christian living are taught in this powerful school. It has been called a "shrine where the will of God is enthroned and love reigns supreme, a sacred place." [8] The images of home in the minds of great men and women lead them to return for renewal to the place of birth and childhood.

When a great man or woman is no longer alive, we often acknowledge the place of their birth and childhood by making a museum site or monument of the home. We then search the spot for indications of the life that occurred therein to make them worthy of notice.

One such home is the Alcott home in Sudbury, Massachusetts. It speaks to each visitor of a quality of life within the home designed to nurture greatness. Louisa May Alcott herself wrote a tribute to one member of the household, her mother:

> Faith that withstood the shocks of toil and time;
>> Hope that defied despair;
>> Patience that conquered care;
> And loyalty, whose courage was sublime;
> The great deep heart that was a home for all—
>> Just, eloquent, and strong
>> In protest against wrong;
> Wide charity, that knew no sin, no fall;
> The Spartan spirit that made life so grand,
>> Mating poor daily needs
>> With high, heroic deeds,
> That wrested happiness from Fate's hard hand. [9]

"In every house should be a window toward the sky." [10]

"The wider a man's horizon is, the greater is the need to be attached to a place." [11] Paul Tournier said this when making his point that every person needs a concrete place because existence is concrete. Home is this place of real community for many. It is this need that gives rise to the expression "there's no place like home." [12]

"Tranquility on the part of the parent in charge is perhaps the most important key to peace and order in the home...." [13]

RELATIONSHIPS

Never speak sharply to an older man, but plead with
him respectfully just as though he were your own father.
Talk to the younger men as you would to much loved
brothers. Treat the older women as mothers, and the
girls as your sisters, thinking only pure thoughts about
them.

1 Timothy 5:1, 2

RELATING WITHIN THE FAMILY

Don't hate your brother. . . . — Leviticus 19:17

"Tell them to be honest and fair—and not to take bribes—and to be merciful and kind to everyone." — Zechariah 7:9

Then Peter came to him and asked, "Sir, how often should I forgive a brother who sins against me? Seven times?"
"No!" Jesus replied, "seventy times seven!" — Matthew 18:21, 22

Don't just pretend that you love others: really love them. Hate what is wrong. Stand on the side of the good. Love each other with brotherly affection and take delight in honoring each other. — Romans 12:9, 10

Be glad for all God is planning for you. Be patient in trouble, and prayerful always. When God's children are in need, you be the one to help them out. And get into the habit of inviting guests home for dinner or, if they need lodging, for the night. — Romans 12:12, 13

If someone mistreats you because you are a Christian, don't curse him; pray that God will bless him. When others are happy, be happy with them. If they are sad, share their sorrow. Work happily together. Don't try to act big. Don't try to get into the good graces of important people, but enjoy the company of ordinary folks. And don't think you know it all! — Romans 12:14–16

Never speak sharply to an older man, but plead with him respectfully just as though he were your own father. Talk to the younger men as you would to much loved brothers. Treat the older women as mothers, and the girls as your sisters, thinking only pure thoughts about them. — 1 Timothy 5:1, 2

The church should take loving care of women whose husbands have died, if they don't have anyone else to help them. But if they have children or grandchildren, these are the ones who should take the responsibility, for kindness should begin at home, supporting needy parents. This is something that pleases God very much. — 1 Timothy 5:3, 4

But anyone who won't care for his own relatives when they need help, especially those living in his own family, has no right to say he is a Christian. Such a person is worse than the heathen. — 1 Timothy 5:8

INSTRUCTIONS TO CHILDREN ABOUT THE TREATMENT OF PARENTS

Deuteronomy 5:16	" 'Honor your father and mother (remember, this is a commandment of the Lord your God); if you do so, you shall have a long, prosperous life in the land he is giving you.' "
Proverbs 30:11, 12, 17	There are those who curse their father and mother, and feel themselves faultless despite their many sins. . . . A man who mocks his father and despises his mother shall have his eye plucked out by ravens and eaten by vultures.
Proverbs 20:20	God puts out the light of the man who curses his father or mother.
Proverbs 23:19, 22–25	O my son, be wise and stay in God's paths. . . . Listen to your father's advice and don't despise an old mother's experience. Get the facts at any price, and hold on tightly to all the good sense you can get. The father of a godly man has cause for joy—what pleasure a wise son is! So give your parents joy!
Mark 7:10–12	"For instance, Moses gave you this law from God: 'Honor your father and mother.' And he said that anyone who speaks against his father or mother must die. But you say it is perfectly all right for a man to disregard his needy parents, telling them, 'Sorry, I can't help you! For I have given to God what I could have given to you.' And so you break the law of God in order to protect your man-made tradition."
Luke 2:51, 52	Then he returned to Nazareth with them and was obedient to them; and his mother stored away all these things in her heart. So Jesus grew both tall and wise, and was loved by God and man.
Ephesians 6:1–3	Children, obey your parents; this is the right thing to do because God has placed them in authority over you. Honor your father and mother. This is the first of God's Ten Commandments that ends with a promise. And this is the promise: that if you honor your father and mother, yours will be a long life, full of blessing.
Colossians 3:20	You children must always obey your fathers and mothers, for that pleases the Lord.

THE GREATEST CHALLENGE IN THE HOME

"God instituted family life to meet our needs, teach us about Himself, and train children for maturity and righteousness." [1]

Leo Tolstoy began his famous novel *Anna Karenina* with the statement that "all happy families resemble one another; every unhappy family is unhappy in its own fashion." The resemblance is in the area of relating to one another.

Our greatest acts of courtesy and tenderness belong to our family more than to strangers. Relating with this principle in mind will help us keep family relationships smooth.

"God transforms us, our marriage, and our children only after we really believe Him! . . . By believing God's Word and really practicing it in daily living, the changes and the exchanges are truly miraculous. Husband and wife, mother and daughter, father and son, even community and job relations are sharply altered and changed by believing." [2]

Many parents who have not experienced good relationships within their own homes may need a communal setting before marriage in order to acquire skills in communicating. Otherwise poor communication patterns are propagated into the new home and family. The church can provide this setting and some re-education as couples planning marriage submit to group or individual training in what might be called "straight talk." This talk is free of games and hidden things. In the Christian home our talk needs to build and not destroy family members.

"It is only through the process of reconciliation with our parents that we finally learn how to accept less than unconditional love—an unavoidable condition of life—with grace." [3]

"With our parents, we must separate from them psychologically, with all the anger and guilt that that implies, while still valuing our connectedness with them on an adult level." [4]

No human relationship is so hopelessly broken that it can't be mended. Healing begins with two words: *I'm sorry.*

"When a child sees or hears his parents fighting or quarreling, satisfaction of his safety needs is impeded. Even though a parent does not turn on the child as a compensatory retaliation for failure to attack or fight back with the spouse, as sometimes does happen, the child feels that his world is threatened. Chronic parental incompatibility may easily be a major contributor to crippling anxiety. When the child hears talk about divorce, separation, or even temporarily "taking off," his safety is menaced and fear and dread preclude his freely taking part in play. He seems to feel that if he stays close by his parents neither one will leave. He cannot attend to his tasks at school because of the threat of absence of one or the other of his parents.

"Lacking the maturity for discrimination, some children pick out just a few words of the quarrel and, hearing their own name, seem to internalize the belief that somehow they have caused the turmoil."[5]

"In the teen years, rebellion against authority and convention is to be expected and tolerated for the sake of learning and growth . . . no matter how wise we are, we cannot be right for any length of time in our teenagers' eyes . . . the beginning of wisdom is silence; the second stage is listening."[6]

"The central theme of adolescence is that of identity, coming to know who one is, what one believes in and values, what one wants to accomplish and get out of life. The adolescent has to come to terms with a new kind of body with new potentialities for feeling and acting, and to rearrange his or her self-image accordingly. Corresponding to changes in his body there emerges a whole new constellation of meanings in the life space. The adolescent's new and often confused self-awareness—manifested largely as self-consciousness—involves a new push for independence."[7] Relating to this changing individual within the home setting involves a great deal of caring and stretching on the part of parents.

Parents play various roles at each stage of their child's development. Some advice given to parents of teens in a casual talk was:

> Seem sure of yourself.
> Keep on truckin'.
> Prepare for ego blows, the descent of friends,
>   and the revelations.[8]

All the idiosyncrasies of parents that pique us as adolescents endear our parents to us as we recall them in our old age. Time changes things.

LOVE

. . . you have been given freedom: not freedom to do wrong, but freedom to love and serve each other. For the whole Law can be summed up in this one command: "Love others as you love yourself."

Galatians 5:13, 14

HARMONY WILL RESULT FROM LOVE EXPRESSED

"Stay there with him awhile until your brother's fury is spent, and he forgets what you have done. Then I will send for you. For why should I be bereaved of both of you in one day?"

Genesis 27:44, 45

May God who gives patience, steadiness, and encouragement help you to live in complete harmony with each other—each with the attitude of Christ toward the other.

Romans 15:5

. . .you have been given freedom: not freedom to do wrong, but freedom to love and serve each other. For the whole Law can be summed up in this one command: "Love others as you love yourself."

Galatians 5:13, 14

But when the Holy Spirit controls our lives he will produce this kind of fruit in us: love, joy, peace, patience, kindness, goodness, faithfulness, gentleness and self-control. . . .

Galatians 5:22, 23

Instead, be kind to each other, tenderhearted, forgiving one another, just as God has forgiven you because you belong to Christ.

Ephesians 4:32

Honor Christ by submitting to each other.

Ephesians 5:21

Continue to love each other with true brotherly love.

Hebrews 13:1

Dear friends, let us practice loving each other, for love comes from God and those who are loving and kind show that they are the children of God, and that they are getting to know him better. But if a person isn't loving and kind, it shows that he doesn't know God—for God is love.

1 John 4:7, 8

If anyone says "I love God," but keeps on hating his brother, he is a liar; for if he doesn't love his brother who is right there in front of him, how can he love God whom he has never seen? And God himself has said that one must love not only God, but his brother too.

1 John 4:20, 21

THE LIVING FAMILY LOVES

> There is beauty all around
> When there's love at home;
> There is joy in every sound
> When there's love at home.
>
> Peace and plenty here abide,
> Smiling sweet on every side;
> Time doth softly, sweetly glide
> When there's love at home.[1]

"Love is being open, respectful, and caring enough to really hear the other person's feelings. It's being a real person to him or to her. That is the Jesus-style of living." [2]

The language of love is not the language of our choice. If it is effective in saying, "I love you," it is the language that the other person can hear. When the lights go on inside the other person and they respond with, "Yes, you do love me," we can know that we have spoken the language of love. For some, it is touch; for others, help with a task; and for many, it is simply saying, "I love you." In other words, doing dishes for your wife or buying bubble gum for your son may not be the best language for them to hear.

"All loves should be simply stepping-stones to the love of God. So it was with me; and blessed be his name for his great goodness and mercy." [3]

"Love, it has been said, flows downward. The love of parents for their children has always been far more powerful than that of children for their parents; and who among the sons of men ever loved God with a thousandth part of the love which God has manifested to us?" [4]

Inner discipline for a child requires teaching, trusting and risking a great deal on the part of a parent or teacher. The child grows strong inside as the parent pays this threefold price: the cost of loving.

Love unites rather than separates. Love which results in strong family unity will erect an impenetrable wall against hostile forces. Try to come up against a family that is strongly united and you will see!

"The Christian home rests on an invisible foundation. It consists of love and adherence to the Word of God. Relationships are limited and unique but love is universal. If you love God, you will love others. Without love, the intimacies of the marriage relationship can drive you and your marriage partner into separate paths. To demonstrate your love for God, you must obey His commands. This will lead you to a serious study of God's Word. As you apply the precepts of His Word to your life, you will develop the characteristics required for good home life." [5]

Love, as demonstrated in the Godhead, can be expressed daily in the family setting. Daily, the man has opportunities to give to his mate in the manner in which Christ gave up His very life for His Bride. Daily, the woman can express her faithfulness to her husband in purity and service, just as the Church to Christ. And daily, the children can express their love in obeying their parents as Christ obeyed His heavenly Father, perfectly doing His will in all things. Does the Christian family have any option but to love in this manner? Or any greater privilege!

"Love is an emotion that gives meaning and helpful purpose to relationships. It is a function of empathy and identification. We sense another person's feelings by empathy; as we identify with those feelings, we care about what is happening to that person as though it were happening to us. Love desires the same benefit for the other person as one would wish for himself. Love is an emotion whose dominant feeling is affection. The goal of love is the close association of another person with oneself." [6]

"It is important to bear in mind this timeless truth. Love is consonant with our emotional nature. All effects of loving relationships are beneficial and become a permanent part of the psyche. In other words, feelings of love cannot be externalized so that one feels less loving because he has expressed love. On the contrary, expressing love tends to increase and enrich the love that is felt." [7]

"Loving God with our total self according to the first great commandment settles once and for all our search for self-identity. We know who we are: we are His, and we belong to Him. We know what we are: we are good and acceptable, for He has atoned for our sins. We know why we are: we have a good destiny, being created in His image and for His glory to live forever with Him." [8]

GENTLENESS

But the wisdom that comes from heaven is first of all
pure and full of quiet gentleness. Then it is peace-loving
and courteous. It allows discussion and is willing to yield
to others; it is full of mercy and good deeds. It is wholehearted and straightforward and sincere. And those who
are peacemakers will plant seeds of peace and reap a
harvest of goodness.

James 3:17, 18

GENTLENESS IS BEST LEARNED IN FAMILIES

He is like a father to us, tender and sympathetic to those who reverence him.

Psalms 103:13

Gentle words cause life and health; griping brings discouragement.

Proverbs 15:4

Kind words are like honey—enjoyable and healthful.

Proverbs 16:24

A cheerful heart does good like medicine, but a broken spirit makes one sick.

Proverbs 17:22

"Wear my yoke—for it fits perfectly—and let me teach you; for I am gentle and humble, and you shall find rest for your souls; for I give you only light burdens."

Matthew 11:29, 30

The Kingdom of God is not just talking; it is living by God's power. Which do you choose? Shall I come with punishment and scolding, or shall I come with quiet love and gentleness?

1 Corinthians 4:20, 21

But we were as gentle among you as a mother feeding and caring for her own children.

1 Thessalonians 2:7

Remind your people. . . . They must not speak evil of anyone, nor quarrel, but be gentle and truly courteous to all.

Titus 3:1, 2

Dear brothers, if a Christian is overcome by some sin, you who are godly should gently and humbly help him back onto the right path. . . .

Galatians 6:1

Be beautiful inside, in your hearts, with the lasting charm of a gentle and quiet spirit which is so precious to God.

1 Peter 3:4

But the wisdom that comes from heaven is first of all pure and full of quiet gentleness. Then it is peace-loving and courteous. It allows discussion and is willing to yield to others; it is full of mercy and good deeds. It is wholehearted and straightforward and sincere. And those who are peacemakers will plant seeds of peace and reap a harvest of goodness.

James 3:17, 18

SUCCESSFUL CHILD REARING
NEEDS GENTLENESS

"There is no formula for successful child rearing; the closest thing to an effective key is consistency with gentleness." [1]

Since gentleness is the "treatment or behavior toward whatever is precious, fragile, and vulnerable," one is more inclined to be gentle with children and pets than with adult persons. Yet adults crave gentle care.

> Gentle as a kitten's eyes,
> Gentle as a warm spring breeze,
> Gentle as a May raindrop,
> Gentle as a slender brook,
> Gentle as a harpsichord,
> Gentle as a falling feather,
> Gentle as a baby's coo,
> And, hopefully, a gentle you.

Just inside the door of home a blanket of gentleness should cover each member—gentleness inside my doors. In a time when pressure drives some human beings to the limit, we need to find gentleness inside the home.

Gentleness is the velvet and satin of life that smooths things out and gives the moments of living rich quality.

To live like Jesus is to live gently. Both in inner gentleness of thought and feeling and in the outer gentleness of word and action, we reflect Christ.

"Nothing is so strong as gentleness; nothing so gentle as real strength." [2]

"True gentleness is founded on a sense of what we owe to Him who made us, and to the common nature which we all share. It arises from reflection on our own failings and wants, and from just views of the condition and duty of man." [3]

A home that is filled with gentleness sends out members who are gentle with humanity. Their view is expansive because they gain God's viewpoint on mankind and nature—a gentle, tolerant view grown up in the home.

A starting point for being gentle with others is to be gentle with yourself. Because you are deeply loved by God however and wherever He finds you, you can be gentle with yourself.

Gentleness doesn't mean one is never angry. It means that anger is not used to destroy another person.

GROWTH

Don't let anyone think little of you because you are
young. Be their ideal; let them follow the way you teach
and live; be a pattern for them in your love, your faith,
and your clean thoughts.

1 Timothy 4:12

LEARNING TO GROW IS DONE BEST IN THE FAMILY

A wise youth accepts his father's rebuke; a young mocker doesn't.

Proverbs 13:1

My son, how I will rejoice if you become a man of common sense. Yes, my heart will thrill to your thoughtful, wise words.

Proverbs 23:15, 16

Any enterprise is built by wise planning, becomes strong through common sense, and profits wonderfully by keeping abreast of the facts.

Proverbs 24:3, 4

Young man, it's wonderful to be young! Enjoy every minute of it! Do all you want to; take in everything, but realize that you must account to God for everything you do. So banish grief and pain, but remember that youth, with a whole life before it, can make serious mistakes. Don't let the excitement of being young cause you to forget about your Creator. Honor him in your youth before the evil years come—when you'll no longer enjoy living.

Ecclesiastes 11:9–12:1

Yes, remember your Creator now while you are young, before the silver cord of life snaps, and the golden bowl is broken, and the pitcher is broken at the fountain, and the wheel is broken at the cistern; and the dust returns to the earth as it was, and the spirit returns to God who gave it.

Ecclesiastes 12:6, 7

But this precious treasure—this light and power that now shine within us—is held in a perishable container, that is, in our weak bodies. Everyone can see that the glorious power within must be from God and is not our own.

2 Corinthians 4:7

That is why we never give up. Though our bodies are dying, our inner strength in the Lord is growing every day.

2 Corinthians 4:16

1 Timothy 4:7–9

Don't waste time arguing over foolish ideas and silly myths and legends. Spend your time and energy in the exercise of keeping spiritually fit. Bodily exercise is all right, but spiritual exercise is much more important and is a tonic for all you do. So exercise yourself spiritually and practice being a better Christian, because that will help you not only now in this life, but in the next life too. This is the truth and everyone should accept it.

1 Timothy 4:12

Don't let anyone think little of you because you are young. Be their ideal; let them follow the way you teach and live; be a pattern for them in your love, your faith, and your clean thoughts.

FAMILY GROWTH BY BEING TOGETHER

Last of all I want to remind you that your strength must come from the Lord's mighty power within you. Put on all of God's armor so that you will be able to stand safe against all strategies and tricks of Satan. For we are not fighting against people made of flesh and blood, but against persons without bodies—the evil rulers of the unseen world, those mighty satanic beings and great evil princes of darkness who rule this world; and against huge numbers of wicked spirits in the spirit world. So use every piece of God's armor to resist the enemy whenever he attacks, and when it is all over, you will still be standing up. But to do this, you will need the strong belt of truth and the breastplate of God's approval. Wear shoes that are able to speed you on as you preach the Good News of peace with God. In every battle you will need faith as your shield to stop the fiery arrows aimed at you by Satan. And you will need the helmet of salvation and the sword of the Spirit—which is the Word of God.

Ephesians 6:10–17

Always be full of joy in the Lord; I say it again, rejoice! Let everyone see that you are unselfish and considerate in all you do. Remember that the Lord is coming soon. Don't worry about anything; instead, pray about everything; tell God your needs and don't forget to thank him for his answers. If you do this you will experience God's peace, which is far more wonderful than the human mind can understand. His peace will keep your thoughts and your hearts quiet and at rest as you trust in Christ Jesus. And now, brothers, as I close this letter let me say this one more thing: Fix your thoughts on what is true and good and right. Think about things that are pure and lovely, and dwell on the fine, good things in others. Think about all you can praise God for and be glad about.

Philippians 4:4–8

Together in Worship

And no one can ever lay any other real foundation than that one we already have—Jesus Christ.

1 Corinthians 3:11

And so, dear brothers, now we may walk right into the very Holy of Holies where God is, because of the blood of Jesus. This is the fresh, new, life-giving way which Christ has opened up for us by tearing the curtain—his human body—to

Hebrews 10:19–25

let us into the holy presence of God. And since this great High Priest of ours rules over God's household, let us go right in, to God himself, with true hearts fully trusting him to receive us, because we have been sprinkled with Christ's blood to make us clean, and because our bodies have been washed with pure water. Now we can look forward to the salvation God has promised us. There is no longer any room for doubt, and we can tell others that salvation is ours, for there is no question that he will do what he says. In response to all he has done for us, let us outdo each other in being helpful and kind to each other and in doing good. Let us not neglect our church meetings, as some people do, but encourage and warn each other, especially now that the day of his coming back again is drawing near.

Together in Daily Living

1 Peter 3:8–12

And now this word to all of you: You should be like one big happy family, full of sympathy toward each other, loving one another with tender hearts and humble minds. Don't repay evil for evil. Don't snap back at those who say unkind things about you. Instead, pray for God's help for them, for we are to be kind to others, and God will bless us for it. If you want a happy, good life, keep control of your tongue, and guard your lips from telling lies. Turn away from evil and do good. Try to live in peace even if you must run after it to catch and hold it! For the Lord is watching his children, listening to their prayers. . . .

Growth is an ingredient of any successful marriage. Tournier wrote that the "true meaning of marriage is an incessant exchange in which each is encouraged to excel himself." [1]

"A woman whom one has watched growing old is never old." [2]

"For if there is any responsibility in the cycle of life it must be that one generation owes to the rest that strength by which it can come to face ultimate concerns in its own way—unmarred by debilitating poverty or by the neurotic concerns caused by emotional exploitation." [3]

"We need to accept that there are limits and learn how to internalize them and pass them on in such a way that we can set our own controls and our own ideals and be autonomous without being isolated." [4]

"Fortunate the child who has the guidance of parents who are themselves grown up—parents who do not play for his attention when he is busily and profitably employed—parents who do not relieve their own pent-up feelings by punishing him—parents who above everything else do not punish him by withdrawing their companionship, a procedure which is probably more destructive than any other one thing which is often done. Fortunate indeed the child whose parents have the self-control they expect of him—parents who are themselves serene and well poised, who are consistent, who are reasonable, who are always honest and frank with him—parents who treat him with fine respect and consideration—parents who above all surround him with a deep, abiding, and wise affection, of which he is always certain, and in which from babyhood on he is always secure." [5]

"Praise does wonders in child nurture. If mother or teacher sees only the child's faults, soon he may not care to try. Praise the desirable and ignore the undesirable and the latter will not be practiced long. Faultfinding, complaining of the bad conduct, scolding, harping, nagging—all these call attention to misbehavior or the undesirable. Approve any conduct that you know required his self-decision and self-direction." [6]

Paul Tournier classified persons as strong or weak in their reaction to life situations. In relation to a child, he wrote, "A child's reactions, strong or weak, usually become established and persist throughout all of life." [7] Growth in adulthood would move one to balance reactions in order to respond to each situation appropriately.

"Whatever his religion, every American child is taught something akin to the Christian ethic, stressing such virtues as charity, forbearance, compassion, altruism, humility, and cooperation, and corresponding to an attitude of basic trust, perhaps with an ascetic overtone. But he also learns the American business ethic of dog eat dog, the survival of the fittest, which stresses and demands such traits as aggression, competitiveness, acquisitiveness, self-preservation, guile, and ruthlessness." [8]

"Adolescents are, more than anything else, growing up—and they will not do it quietly. They will not stay in their room and do their growing in isolation; they will not restrict their growing to the times when they are safely among peers. Their growing spills out, unsystematically, all over the place. But in this way adolescents, energetically modeling and insistently stimulating growth, are God's gift to parents who are in danger of being arrested in their own growth.

"Parents can of course, even in the face of this, refuse to grow. They can say, 'I have completed my growing up; I know what it means to be a person, a Christian, a citizen, a man, a woman. And I am going to preside over your growing up, I will provide the guidelines, I will make the rules, I will determine the course of your growth.' Such a position can be either benevolent or despotic, but it is, in either case, detached. The parents have removed themselves from the processes of growth and only observe and preside over the growth of the child. Or the parents can disqualify themselves from further growth by saying, 'I've made such a mess of my own growing up that I am not going to share in yours. . . .' The stance may appear to be full of humility and modesty; in effect, it is a capitulation to despair. . . .

"Parents of adolescents, it seems to me, are not best characterized as people who do the right things or say the right things, but as ones who plunge into the process of growth. . . .

"The task of the parent, in other words, is not directly to confront the problems of the young and find the best solutions to them. It is to confront life, and Christ in life, and deal with that. A parent's main job is not to be a parent but be a person. . . . The parent's main task is to give a living demonstration that adulthood is full, alive, and Christian." [9]

CELEBRATIONS

"But his father said to the slaves, 'Quick! Bring the finest robe in the house and put it on him. And a jeweled
ring for his finger; and shoes! And kill the calf we have
in the fattening pen. We must celebrate with a feast, for
this son of mine was dead and has returned to life. He
was lost and is found.' So the party began."

Luke 15:22–24

RITUAL AND CELEBRATION LEND STRENGTH TO FAMILY LIFE

" 'And now, O Lord, see, I have brought you a token of the first of the crops from the ground you have given me.' Then place the samples before the Lord your God, and worship him. Afterwards, go and feast on all the good things he has given you. Celebrate with your family and with any Levites or migrants living among you."

Deuteronomy 26:10, 11

Every year when each of Job's sons had a birthday, he invited his brothers and sisters to his home for a celebration. On these occasions they would eat and drink with great merriment. When these birthday parties ended—and sometimes they lasted several days—Job would summon his children to him and sanctify them, getting up early in the morning and offering a burnt offering for each of them. For Job said, "Perhaps my sons have sinned and turned away from God in their hearts." This was Job's regular practice.

Job 1:4, 5

"But his father said to the slaves, 'Quick! Bring the finest robe in the house and put it on him. And a jeweled ring for his finger; and shoes! And kill the calf we have in the fattening pen. We must celebrate with a feast, for this son of mine was dead and has returned to life. He was lost and is found.' So the party began."

Luke 15:22–24

WORSHIP IN THE FAMILY

"From the services in which I joined as a child I have taken with me into life a feeling for what is solemn, and a need for self-recollection, without which I cannot realize the meaning of my life. I cannot, therefore, support the opinion of those who would not let children take part in grown-up people's services till they to some extent understand them. The important thing is not that they shall understand but that they shall feel something of what is serious and solemn. The fact that a child sees his elders full of devotion, and has to feel something of devotion himself, that is what gives the service meaning for him." [1]

"Adults represent God to children by everything they say and do." [2]

A family ritual is the way a family acts out the importance of a belief at a certain time of the day or year. A break in everyday routine for such a ritual will cement beliefs into the growing child which can seldom be reversed.

"Success in family altar is more a matter of conviction than a matter of technique or carefully, well-chosen material." [3]

Family worship is more helpful to a child's growth than the best of sermons and the finest of Sunday schools. "Family worship is the total sum of a father's and mother's relationship to each other, to their children, and to God." [4]

"Every family needs to have its own traditions. . . . We have our annual Winter Picnic. . . . Another family tradition is this: each spring the first person to find a wild violet and bring it home has a cake baked for him. . . . These private traditions seem to help unite the family by giving them certain experiences a bit different from others they have in common with the rest of society." [5]

"Our religious life was especially family-centered. I fondly recall many family rituals, a number of which were centered around the dinner table. Dinner itself was a sort of ritual. . . . Among the rituals centered around the dinner table was Advent, the preparation for Christmas. . . . Ritual was important in my parents' house only as it involved each of us. . . ." [6]

THE LIVING FAMILY CELEBRATES TRADITIONAL HOLIDAYS

Thanksgiving

"They are going home for Thanksgiving, traveling through clogged arteries of airports and highways, bearing bridge chairs and serving plates, Port-a-Cribs, and pies. They are going home to rooms that resound with old arguments and interruptions, to piano benches filled with small cousins, to dining-room tables stretched out to the last half.

"They no longer migrate over the river and through the woods. . . .

"Thanksgiving isn't just a feast but a reunion. It's no longer a celebration of food (which is plentiful in America) but of family, which is scarce.

"The family may be the one social glue strong enough to withstand the centrifuge of special interests which send us spinning away from each other.

"Our families are not just the people (if I may massacre Robert Frost) who 'when you have to go there, They have to take you in.' They are the people who maintain an unreasonable interest in each other. They are the natural peacemakers in the generation war." [7]

Christmas

Peter Marshall, in a sermon, said, "We want to hold on to the old customs and traditions because they strengthen our family ties, bind us to our friends, make us one with mankind for whom the Child was born . . . so we will not 'spend' Christmas, nor 'observe' Christmas. We will 'keep' Christmas—keep it as it is—in all the loveliness of its ancient traditions. May we keep it in our hearts that we may be kept in its hope." [8]

Macy's Thanksgiving Day parade heralds the Christmas season. Here again. What can make it more meaningful for our family this year? More atmosphere—firelight and pine scent? More parties with friends? More presents—birthstone rings, argyle sweaters, golf clubs?

Mankind seems to be longing for something at this time annually. Gathering in malls, churches, and even bars, they search—perhaps for reality. And they are very close. In fact, Christmas is one time of the year when American family tradition focuses on the reason and source of existence. Families sing about love coming down, see dramas about God's Son becoming man, and create works of art about the miracle of a simple birth to solve man's dilemma. Truth lies at the core of the Christmas celebration. Thus, when we gather to recall the Bethlehem event each winter, we come close to the truth. There is hope in living because of God's gift to the human family.

Yet, in coming so close, we can be even more distant. "So near and yet so far." We calculate our giving. We overspend for everything instead of giving ourselves. We are pressured to "beat the twenty-fifth." In all of this, we submerge what is real. To correct this for our family this year, first, planned times of thought and worship will need to be central in our celebration. Second, expressing our love to those who need it most will emulate our Lord's Christmas behavior. From slavery to our shopping list, we can move to sacrificing ourselves to needy persons.

Only a "grinch" fails to enjoy the sentimental symbols expressed in lights, color, and sound. Only the fool, however, thinks that this is the meaning of Christmas and its long endurance in American tradition. It all remains central to American family life in the winter season, because Jesus' coming was the expression of God's love to a world desperately lost without it. Let us share Christmas in its reality.

One would be in less danger
From the wiles of the stranger
If one's own kin and kith
Were more fun to be with.[9]

"Family jokes, though rightly cursed by strangers, are the bond that keeps most families alive." [10]

"Our children need to acquire perspective with a sense of humor and humility. Laughter is the safety valve of most human beings. Because we are capable of laughter, we see ourselves in perspective to others and to unattainable ideals, and we appreciate the variety of routes by which we seek our goals and develop compassion for others. By learning to laugh at ourselves, to laugh at our failings and our idiosyncrasies, we learn to understand frailties and shortcomings in others.

"The ability to share amusing experiences and to communicate nonverbalized signs of understanding is an important tool to acquire. The sparkle in the eye, the wink, the giggle, the deep-throated laugh, are tools of the entire human family. Such spontaneous gestures of understanding can do more to break down barriers than long dissertations on friendship and love." [11]

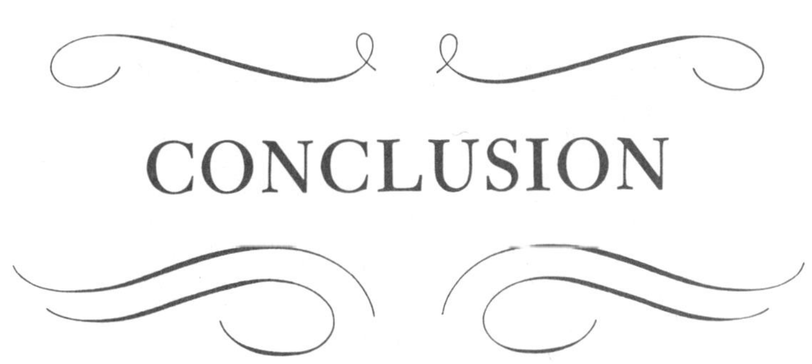

CONCLUSION

And now this word to all of you: You should be like one big happy family, full of sympathy toward each other, loving one another with tender hearts and humble minds. Don't snap back at those who say unkind things about you. Instead, pray for God's help for them, for we are to be kind to others, and God will bless us for it. If you want a happy, good life, keep control of your tongue, and guard your lips from telling lies. Turn away from evil and do good. Try to live in peace even if you must run after it and hold it! For the Lord is watching his children, listening to their prayers. . . .

1 Peter 3:8–12

"The ties of family and of country were never intended to circumscribe the soul. If allowed to become exclusive, engrossing, clannish, so as to shut out the general claims of the human race, the highest end of Providence is frustrated, and home, instead of being the nursery, becomes the grave of the heart." [1]

"The family was intended by God to be the basic unit of society. It was from this unit that society was to draw its strength, its fidelity, its God-consciousness, and its instruction as to the nature of God and His will. The family was where we are to derive, experience, and practice the blessings of obedience to divine principles and truths. I suppose, if we would trace the history of our own decaying social structure and its moral and spiritual disintegration, we would find that our society's decline runs parallel to the fragmentation of marriage and family in our current social life-style and concepts. Also, if we could accurately determine the cause of the moral and spiritual decline and fall of historical civilizations, it is most likely we would find the same pairing of causes." [2]

"Does good parenting guarantee good children? A lot of parents assume that it does: that if we do a responsible and intelligent job as mothers and fathers, if we provide a Christian home and are faithful in our prayers, if we raise our children 'in the nurture and admonition of the Lord,' our children are going to turn out well.

"But there are precious few facts to support the assumption. One does not have to look around very long to observe some simply magnificent people who come from absolutely wretched homes. And some very troubled people who have been reared in stable, responsible, Christian homes. Even allowing for the fact that appearances are misleading—that the alcoholic father and the prostitute mother really 'had a heart of gold'—which accounts for the fact that their son is a kindly, successful physician; and the 'pillar of the church' parents were first-class Pharisees and had a most deserved comeuppance in the sordid miseries of their daughter—still, there are enough exceptions to 'good parents produce good children' that it can hardly be held as a comfortable truth.

"This doesn't relieve parents from doing as good a job as possible in rearing their children. Christian parents are under solemn command to treat the children God has given them lovingly, responsibly, and seriously. But rewards are not guaranteed. And it doesn't mean that what parents do doesn't have an enormous effect on children, for it does. Good parents are an incalculable asset. Still, there are no guarantees. The finest parents in the world are no sure protection against youth's making unwise decisions or evil choices.

"Christians are not determinists." [3]

NOTES

Family

1. From the Montreal Committee of Family Life and Parent Education, Report of 1955, p. 190.
2. Edith Schaeffer, "What Is a Family?" Pamphlet from the Continental Congress on the Family, Saint Louis, Missouri, 1975.
3. Gabriel Moran, *Education Toward Adulthood* (Ramsay, N.J.: the Paulist Press, 1979), p. 83.
4. Ibid.
5. Howard Clinebell, *Mental Health Through Christian Community* (Nashville: Abingdon Press, 1965), p. 209.
6. Pope Leo XIII.
7. Jean Paul Richter.
8. Clifford Kirkpatrick, *The Family* (New York: The Ronald Press, 1955).
9. Gloria Gaither, "Caution: Home Zone," *Today's Christian Woman* (Fall 1982), p. 77.
10. John Bowring.
11. Lord Houghton.
12. Jay Adams, *Christian Living in the Home* (Grand Rapids, Mich.: Baker Book House, 1972).
13. Larry Christensen, *The Christian Family* (Minneapolis: Bethany Fellowship, 1970).
14. Norman H. Wright. Talk delivered at Canadian Bible College, Regina, Saskatchewan, Canada.
15. Cliff Schimmels, *How to Help Your Child Survive and Thrive in Public School* (Old Tappan, N.J.: Fleming H. Revell Company, 1982), pp. 80–85.
16. Gracie Chapman, "His, Mine . . . Ours," *Good Housekeeping* magazine (November 1982), p. 104.

Parents

1. Gladys Hunt, "Ten Guidelines to a Happy Family," *Moody Monthly* (June 1973), p. 22.
2. Bernard Meltzer, *Bernard Meltzer's Guidance for Living* (New York: Dial Press, Mellan Associates, Inc., 1982).
3. Larry Richards, *A New Face for the Church* (Grand Rapids, Mich.: Zondervan Publishing House, 1970).
4. Naomi Feigilson Chase, *A Child Is Being Beaten* (New York: Holt, Rinehart & Winston, 1975).
5. Howard Hendricks. Talk at the Continental Congress on the Family, Saint Louis, Missouri, 1975.
6. J. E. Runions, *What They Did Right*, ed. Virginia Hearn (Wheaton, Ill.: Tyndale House Publishers, 1974).
7. Anne Bradstreet, "Meditations Divine and Moral," *The Works of Anne Bradstreet* (Cambridge: Harvard University Press, 1961), p. 321.
8. Jay Adams, *Christian Living in the Home* (Grand Rapids, Mich.: Baker Book House, 1972).
9. Larry Christensen, *The Christian Family* (Minneapolis: Bethany House Publishers, 1970).
10. James Dobson, *Hide or Seek* (Old Tappan, N.J.: Fleming H. Revell Company, 1974).

11. Kenneth Gangel, *The Family First* (Winona Lake, Ind.: BMH Books, 1972).

12. Howard Hendricks, *Heaven Help the Home!* (Wheaton, Ill.: Victor Books, 1973).

13. Levi Miller, *The Family in Today's Society* Cassette (Scottdale, Pa.: Herald Press, 1972).

14. Maxine Hancock, *People in Process* (Old Tappan, N.J.: Fleming H. Revell Company, 1978), p. 33.

15. Bruce Narramore, *Help! I'm a Parent* (Grand Rapids, Mich.: Zondervan Publishing House, 1972).

16. Drepanius.

17. Ellen Goodman, *Close to Home* (New York: Simon & Schuster, 1979), p. 169.

18. Grace H. Ketterman, M.D., and Herbert L. Ketterman, M.D., *The Complete Book of Baby and Child Care for Christian Parents* (Old Tappan, N.J.: Fleming H. Revell Company, 1982).

19. Cotton Mather, *Bonifacious.*

20. Plato.

21. Fenelon.

22. Bradstreet, "Letter to Son Simon," *Works of Anne Bradstreet.*

23. *Developmental Psychology Today* (New York: Random House, Inc., 1971), pp. 287, 288.

24. Horace Bushnell, *Christian Nurture* (New Haven, Conn.: Yale University Press, 1916), p. 76.

25. Oral tradition.

26. Kahlil Gibran, *The Prophet* (New York: Alfred A. Knopf, Inc., 1923).

27. "The Greatest Educational Force," *Christianity Today* (August 24, 1964), pp. 28, 29.

28. Henry Ward Beecher.

29. Bruce Narramore, "Christian Parenthood in a Modern World," p. 13. Pamphlet from the Continental Congress on the Family, Saint Louis, Missouri, 1975.

30. Ann Landers.

31. Howard Clinebell, *Mental Health Through Christian Community* (Nashville: Abingdon Press, 1965), p. 190.

32. James Dobson. *Hide or Seek* (Old Tappan, N.J.: Fleming H. Revell Company, 1974).

33. Miller, *Family in Today's Society.*

34. Johnny Cash, "My Children Walk in Truth" (Hendersonville, Tenn.: House of Cash, 1974).

Fathers

1. John M. Drescher, "If I Were Starting My Family Again," *Guideposts* magazine (March 1979), pp. 17–24. Originally published by Abingdon Press.

2. Source unknown.

3. Dr. Fitzhugh Dodson, *How to Father* (New York: Signet Books, New American Library, 1975).

4. General Douglas MacArthur, *Reminiscences* (New York: McGraw-Hill Book Company, 1964).

5. Source unknown.

6. Richard Strauss, *Confident Children and How They Grow* (Wheaton, Ill.: Tyndale House Publishers, 1975), pp. 117–127.

7. Ricks L. Falk, "Beatitudes of a Husband and Father," *Decision* magazine (June 1976).

Mothers

1. Richard Strauss, *Confident Children and How They Grow* (Wheaton, Ill.: Tyndale House Publishers, 1975), p. 129.

2. Martin Luther.

3. Lydia H. Sigourney.

4. Oliver Wendell Holmes.

5. Source unknown.

6. Saint Augustine.

7. John S. C. Abbott.

8. Abraham Lincoln.

9. Victor Hugo.

10. Washington Irving.

Children

1. "Affirmation on the Family," Continental Congress on the Family, Saint Louis, Missouri, 1975.

2. Lewis Bird, "My Credo for the Family," *Eternity* magazine (Fall 1977), p. 44.

3. Joseph Joubert.

4. Charles Haddon Spurgeon.

5. Charles Buxton.

6. George Eliot.

7. John Dewey.

8. John Masefield.

9. *Developmental Psychology Today* (New York: Random House, Inc., 1971), p. 131.

10. John Elias, *The Foundations and Practice of Adult Religious Education* (Malabar, Fla.: Robert E. Krieger Publishing Company, 1982), p. 43.

11. John Milton.

12. Henry Thoreau in *Walden.*

13. William Wordsworth.

14. Sophocles.

15. Cicero.

16. Francis Bacon.

17. Paul Tournier, *Learning to Grow Old* (New York: Harper & Row Publishers, Inc., 1973).

18. Alta Mae Erb, *The Christian Nurture of Children* (Scottdale, Pa.: Herald Press, 1955).

19. Jack Fennema, *Nurturing Children in the Lord* (Grand Rapids, Mich.: Baker Book House, 1977), pp. 20–22.

20. Ibid.

21. Bruce Narramore, *Help! I'm a Parent* (Grand Rapids, Mich.: Zondervan Publishing House, 1972), pp. 117, 124, 125.

22. Ibid., p. 146.

Home

1. Mark and Anne Hanchett, "The Triumphs and Trials of Rearing Children," *Stony Brook School Bulletin* (Winter 1981).

2. Katharine Fullerton Gerould.

3. Lord Houghton.

4. Ellen Goodman, *Close to Home* (New York: Simon & Schuster, 1979), pp. 150, 151.

5. S.S. Cohon, *Judaism: A Way of Life* (New York: Schocken Books Inc., 1948).

6. Theodore Roosevelt, *A Treasury of Sermon Illustrations*, ed. Charles Wallis (Nashville: Abingdon Press, 1950).

7. Samuel Johnson.

8. Alta Mae Erb, *The Christian Nurture of Children* (Scottdale, Pa.: Herald Press, 1955).

9. Louisa May Alcott's "Tribute to a Mother."

10. Source unknown.

11. Paul Tournier, *A Place for You* (New York: Harper & Row Publishers, Inc., 1969).

12. John Howard Payne.

13. Maxine Hancock, *People in Process* (Old Tappan, N.J.: Fleming H. Revell Company, 1978), p. 170.

Relationships

1. Bruce Narramore, *Help! I'm a Parent* (Grand Rapids, Mich.: Zondervan Publishing House, 1972).

2. Joyce Landorf, *His Stubborn Love* (Grand Rapids, Mich.: Zondervan Publishing House, 1971).

3. Maxine Schnall, *Limits: A Search for New Values* (New York: Clarkson N. Potter, Inc., 1981), p. 278.

4. Ibid., p. 277.

5. Harold W. Bernard, *Child Development and Learning* (Boston: Allyn and Bacon, Inc., 1973), p. 238.

6. Haim Ginott, *Between Parent and Teenager* (New York: Macmillan Publishing Company, Inc., 1969).

7. L. Joseph Stone and Joseph Church, *Childhood and Adolescence* (New York: Random House, Inc., 1968), p. 437.

8. Source unknown.

Love

1. Source unknown.

2. Levi Miller, *The Family in Today's Society* Cassette (Scottdale, Pa.: Herald Press, 1972).

3. Plato.

4. Augustus W. Hare and Julius Charles.

5. Henry R. Brandt and Homer E. Dowdy, *Building a Christian Home* (Wheaton, Ill.: Scripture Press, 1960).

6. Horace B. English and Ava C. English, *A Comprehensive Dictionary of Psychological and Psychoanalytical Terms* (New York: Longman Inc., 1958), p. 299.

7. Maurice Wagner, *The Sensation of Being Somebody* (Grand Rapids, Mich.: Zondervan Publishing House, 1975), p. 41.

8. Ibid., p. 169.

Gentleness

1. Ted Ward, from a talk given at Canadian Bible College, Regina, Saskatchewan, Canada.

2. Saint Francis de Sales.

3. Hugh Blair.

Growth

1. Paul Tournier, *Learning to Grow Old* (New York: Harper & Row Publishers, Inc., 1973).

2. Ibid.

3. Erik Erikson, *Insight and Responsibility* (New York: W.W. Norton and Company, Inc., 1964).

4. Maxine Schnall, *Limits: A Search for New Values* (New York: Clarkson N. Potter, Inc., 1981).

5. Grace Langdon, *Home Guidance for Young Children* (New York: Harper & Row Publishers, Inc. [John Day], 1931, 1946).

6. Alta Mae Erb, *The Christian Nurture of Children* (Scottdale, Pa.: Herald Press, 1955).

7. Paul Tournier, *To Resist or To Surrender?* (Atlanta, Ga.: John Knox Press, 1964), p. 21.

8. L. Joseph Stone and Joseph Church, *Childhood and Adolescence* (New York: Random House, Inc. 1968), p. 141.

9. Eugene H. Peterson, *Growing Up in Christ* (Atlanta, Ga.: John Knox Press, 1977), pp. 13–15.

Celebrations

1. Albert Schweitzer, *The Philosophy of Civilization* (London: A&C Black Ltd.).

2. Judith Allen Shelly, *The Spiritual Needs of Children* (Downers Grove, Ill.: InterVarsity Press, 1982).

3. Henry R. Brandt and Homer E. Dowdy, *Building a Christian Home* (Wheaton, Ill.: Scripture Press Publications, Inc., 1960).

4. Ken Anderson, *The Family That Makes It* (Wheaton, Ill.: Victor Books, 1971), pp. 101–118.

5. Deborah Bayly, *What They Did Right*, ed. Virginia Hearn (Wheaton, Ill.: Tyndale House Publishers, 1974), p. 25.

6. Anne Fillin, Ibid., pp. 125–127.

7. Ellen Goodman, *Close to Home* (New York: Simon & Schuster, 1979).

8. Peter Marshall, *Let's Keep Christmas* (Lincoln, Va.: Chosen Books, 1953).

9. Ogden Nash.

10. Stella Benson.

11. *Living and Learning.* The Report of the Provincial Committee on Aims and Objectives of Education in the Schools of Ontario, p. 46.

Conclusion

1. William Ellery Channing.

2. Fred Barshaw, "The Church's Role in Healing and Strengthening the Christian Family," *Theology, News and Notes* (December 1974), p. 12.

3. Eugene H. Peterson, *Growing Up in Christ* (Atlanta, Ga.: John Knox Press, 1976), p. 81.